Sanjeev Kapoor's

Chai - Nashta

In association with Alyona Kapoor

Popular Prakashan
www.popularprakashan.com

Published by
POPULAR PRAKASHAN PVT. LTD.
301, Mahalaxmi Chambers
22, Bhulabhai Desai Road
Mumbai - 400 026
for KHANA KHAZANA PUBLICATIONS PVT. LTD.

First Published 2009
Fourth Reprint 2014

(4322)
ISBN: 978-81-7991-574-5

Design: Anjali Sawant

PRINTED IN INDIA
by Saurabh Printers Pvt. Ltd.
A-16, Sector 4, Noida

AUTHOR'S NOTE

A hot cup of tea, a crunchy snack on the side and something sweet to top it off - gourmet bliss! A rainy afternoon, a misty morning, a sunny day at the poolside, a cozy evening with friends, a chilly winter's night, late afternoon with hungry kids just home from school – any time is chai-nashta time!

There are few more soul-satisfying meals than a soothing beverage accompanied by a savoury or sweet treat. Think hot Kanda Bhajias, Crispy Wontons and a substantial Triple-decker Sandwich; or a slice of moist, Zesty Lemon Cake, a Crunchy Peanut Cookie or a delightful dollop of Saeb ka Halwa. And if the amber liquid, is literally not your cup of tea, quench your thirst with a piping hot Badam Doodh, a silky Mango Smoothie or a mint-flavoured Iced-spiced Tea.

So take that well-deserved chai-nashta break, and treat yourself to kuchh garam-kuchh thanda, kuchh namkeen, kuchh meetha!

Happy Cooking!

CONTENTS

KUCHH GARAM-KUCHH THANDA

KUCHH NAMKEEN

KUCHH MEETHA

Kahwa

Ingredients

1 teaspoon *kahwa* tea leaves, crushed

2 green cardamoms

2 inches cinnamon

3 teaspoons sugar

2-3 saffron threads (optional)

4-5 almonds, finely crushed

Method

1. Pound together the green cardamoms and cinnamon to a powder.
2. Pour three cups of water into a pan; add the crushed *kahwa* tea leaves, cardamom-cinnamon powder, sugar and saffron and bring to a boil.
3. Boil for five to six minutes or till the tea turns a pale gold.
4. Strain into individual teacups.
5. Sprinkle the almonds on top and serve hot.

Moroccan Mint Tea

Ingredients

2 teaspoons tea leaves

16 fresh mint leaves

4 lemons, cut into wedges

2 one-inch cinnamon sticks

4 star anise

16 teaspoons caster sugar

Method

1. Place the tea leaves, mint leaves, lemon wedges, cinnamon sticks, star anise and caster sugar in a teapot.
2. Top it up with boiling water and let it brew for about three to four minutes.
3. Stir well to dissolve the sugar.
4. Pour into individual glasses and serve hot.

Masala Chai

Ingredients

4-6 teaspoons tea leaves

1 cup milk

1 teaspoon *Chai Masala* (see alongside)

4 teaspoons sugar

Method

1. Boil three cups of water in a pan. Add the tea leaves, milk, *chai masala* and sugar and bring the mixture to a boil again.
2. Boil for a couple of minutes. Strain and serve piping hot.

Chai Masala

Dry-roast and grind 1 inch cinnamon, 4 green cardamoms, 16 black pepper-corns and ¼ teaspoon grated nutmeg. Sift the powder and store in an airtight container.

Minty Iced-Spiced Tea

Ingredients

15-20 fresh mint leaves + a few sprigs

½ inch ginger, chopped

1 inch cinnamon

5 teaspoons tea leaves

7 tablespoons sugar

3 tablespoons lemon juice

Method

1. Boil five cups of water with the ginger and cinnamon. Add the sugar and tea leaves and boil for one minute.

2. Add eight to ten fresh mint leaves; remove from heat, strain and set aside to cool. Stir in the lemon juice.

3. Pour one cup of the decoction mixed with the remaining mint leaves into an ice tray and freeze to make tea-flavoured ice cubes.

4. Place the remaining decoction in the refrigerator to chill.

5. To serve, pour the chilled tea into individual glasses.

6. Add a few flavoured ice cubes, decorate with sprigs of mint and serve immediately.

Tulsi Ki Chai

Ingredients

12-16 fresh basil leaves

4 teaspoons tea leaves

1 inch fresh ginger, peeled and crushed

3 tablespoons honey

3-4 black peppercorns

Method

1. Place the basil leaves and four and a half cups of water in a deep pan and bring to a boil. Lower heat and simmer for five minutes.
2. Add the tea leaves, ginger, honey and peppercorns and bring to a boil once again.
3. Remove from heat, cover and let the tea infuse for about five minutes.
4. Strain into teacups just before serving.

Iced Papaya Tea

Ingredients

900 ml freshly brewed hot tea

16 tablespoons chopped ripe papaya cubes

Crushed ice, as required

Method

1. Pour the tea into a serving jug and add the papaya cubes. Chill thoroughly.
2. Pour over the crushed ice in tall glasses and serve immediately.

Falooda

Ingredients

3 cups milk

3 tablespoons sugar

1 teaspoon *subza*, soaked

½ packet *falooda*, soaked in warm water

2 tablespoons rose syrup

4 scoops vanilla icecream

10-12 cashew nuts, chopped

Method

1. Heat the milk with the sugar and bring to a boil. Set aside to cool and then refrigerate. Add the soaked *subza* to the milk, stir and chill in the refrigerator.

2. Take four wide-mouthed *falooda* glasses and layer each with half a tablespoon of rose syrup.

3. Pour the milk into each glass, top with two to three tablespoons of *falooda* and a scoop of vanilla icecream. Serve sprinkled with cashew nuts.

Note: 1) Falooda is vermicelli made of arrowroot.

2) Subza is the Hindi word for basil seeds.

Thandai

Ingredients

1½ litres (7½ cups) full cream milk

A few saffron threads

1½ cups sugar

25 almonds, blanched and peeled

20 cashew nuts, soaked

30 pistachios, blanched and peeled

3 tablespoons melon seeds, soaked

3 tablespoons poppy seeds, soaked

1 teaspoon green cardamom seeds

20-25 dried rose petals

1 inch cinnamon

8-10 black peppercorns

Method

1. Bring the milk to a boil in a pan; add the saffron and sugar and simmer for a few minutes. Grind together the almonds, cashew nuts, pistachios, melon seeds and poppy seeds with a little milk to a fine paste.

2. Add the paste to the milk and mix well; simmer for three or four minutes.

3. Grind together the cardamom seeds, rose petals, cinnamon and peppercorns to a fine powder. Add the powder to the milk and mix well. Chill the *thandai* and serve.

Pedewali Meethi Lassi

Ingredients

3 cups yogurt

1 cup sugar

1 cup ice cubes

Fresh cream

4 *malai peda*, grated

Method

1. Process the yogurt and sugar for two minutes in a blender.
2. Add the ice cubes and blend for one minute longer.
3. Pour into serving glasses.
4. Top with the cream, garnish with the grated *peda* and serve chilled.

Mango Smoothie

Ingredients

3 large ripe mangoes, peeled and chopped

1 medium ripe mango, peeled and cut into ½-inch cubes, to garnish

3 cups chilled milk

6 tablespoons chilled yogurt

8 tablespoons sugar

10-12 ice cubes, crushed

Method

1. Place the chopped mangoes in the freezer for a while.
2. Process the chilled mangoes, milk, yogurt, sugar and crushed ice cubes together in a blender.
3. Carefully pour the mixture into individual glasses.
4. Serve chilled, decorated with mango cubes.

Iced Cajun Coffee

Ingredients

4 tablespoons instant coffee powder

4 cups cold full cream milk

4 teaspoons vanilla essence

4 small pinches of cinnamon powder

Crushed ice

Method

1. Process the instant coffee powder, full cream milk and vanilla essence in a blender.
2. Pour over the crushed ice in individual glasses.
3. Sprinkle the cinnamon powder over the top and serve immediately.

Badam Doodh

Ingredients

60 almonds

8 cups milk

A generous pinch of saffron

½ teaspoon green cardamom powder

A pinch of nutmeg powder

12 tablespoons sugar

Method

1. Blanch and peel the almonds. Slice fifteen almonds and grind the rest to a paste.
2. Bring the milk to a boil in a thick-bottomed pan.
3. Lower heat, add the almond paste and simmer for fifteen to twenty minutes.
4. Add the saffron, cardamom powder, nutmeg powder and sugar and mix well.
5. Pour into individual glasses, garnish with sliced almonds and serve hot.

Biscuit Corn Sev Puri

Ingredients

16 cream cracker biscuits

2 large potatoes, boiled and mashed

½ cup sweetcorn kernels, blanched

Salt to taste

¼ teaspoon red chilli powder

2 medium onions, chopped

Chaat masala as required

8-10 teaspoons Green Chutney (page 92)

2 tablespoons Red Chilli-Garlic Chutney (page 92)

8-10 teaspoons Date and Tamarind Chutney (page 92)

1 cup fine *sev*

2 tablespoons chopped fresh coriander

1 small unripe green mango, chopped

Method

1. Arrange four biscuits on each plate.
2. In a separate bowl, mix together the mashed potatoes, corn, salt and chilli powder. Divide into sixteen portions.
3. Place a portion of the potato mixture on each biscuit.

4. Sprinkle the onion and *chaat masala* on top.

5. Drizzle half a teaspoon of green chutney, one-fourth teaspoon of red chilli-garlic chutney and one teaspoon of date and tamarind chutney one over the other on each biscuit.

6. Cover the biscuits with plenty of *sev*. Sprinkle fresh coriander and green mango on top.

7. Serve immediately.

Chef's Tip: Add more red chilli-garlic chutney for a spicier snack.

Bhakarwadi Chaat

Ingredients

1 cup mini *bhakarwadi*

½ cup bean sprouts

Salt to taste

1 cup yogurt

2 medium potatoes, boiled and finely chopped

1 large onion, finely chopped

5 tablespoons Green Chutney (page 92)

3 tablespoons Date And Tamarind Chutney (page 92)

1 teaspoon *chaat masala*

¼ teaspoon red chilli powder

1 teaspoon roasted cumin powder

¼ cup nylon *sev*

2 tablespoons chopped fresh coriander

Method

1. Cook the bean sprouts in one and a half cups of boiling salted water for two or three minutes.
2. Drain, refresh in cold water and set aside.

3. Whisk the yogurt with salt and place in a refrigerator to chill for half an hour.

4. To prepare the *chaat*, arrange the *bhakarwadi* on a large serving plate; top with layers of *moong* sprouts, potatoes, onion and chilled yogurt.

5. Drizzle both the chutneys and sprinkle *chaat masala*, chilli powder, cumin powder and nylon *sev* over the yogurt.

6. Garnish with fresh coriander and serve immediately.

Matki Ussal

Ingredients

1 cup brown gram

3 tablespoons oil

½ teaspoon mustard seeds

6-8 curry leaves

2 medium onions, finely chopped

½ teaspoon turmeric powder

½ teaspoon red chilli powder

1 teaspoon *goda masala*

1 teaspoon jaggery, grated

Salt to taste

A few sprigs of fresh coriander, finely chopped

2 tablespoons grated fresh coconut

Spice paste

1 teaspoon cumin seeds

3-4 green chillies, finely chopped

¼ cup grated fresh coconut

6-7 garlic cloves, finely chopped

Method

1. Clean, wash and soak the brown gram overnight in four cups of water. Drain.

2. To make the spice paste, dry-roast the cumin seeds on a *tawa*. Grind together the roasted cumin seeds, green chillies, coconut and garlic to a fine paste.

3. Heat the oil in a pan; add the mustard seeds and when they begin to splutter add the curry leaves and chopped onion. Sauté the onion, stirring continuously till it turns light golden.

4. Add the paste and cook on medium heat for three to four minutes. Add the turmeric powder, chilli powder, *goda masala*, jaggery and salt. Stir well.

5. Add the drained brown gram, mix well and add enough water to just cover the mixture.

6. Bring to a boil and continue cooking on medium heat, stirring occasionally till the brown gram is cooked.

7. Serve hot garnished with chopped fresh coriander and grated coconut.

Note: Goda Masala is the basic spice-mix in Maharashtrian cuisine.

Batter-Fried Onion Rings

Ingredients

6 extra-large onions

2 cups refined flour

3 tablespoons cornflour

Salt to taste

½ teaspoon white pepper powder

½ teaspoon baking powder

½ cup oil + for deep-frying

Method

1. Cut the onions into thick round slices. Separate the onion slices into rings and select only the large outer rings.
2. Sift together the refined flour, cornflour, salt, white pepper powder and baking powder.
3. Gradually stir in half a cup of oil and one and a quarter cups of water to make a thick batter. Whisk the batter continuously for about five to ten minutes.
4. Heat the oil in a *kadai*. Dip the onion rings in the batter and deep-fry till crisp. Drain on absorbent paper. Serve hot.

Sichuan Vegetable Fingers

Ingredients

1 medium carrot, grated

¼ medium cauliflower, grated

1 small green capsicum, finely chopped

¼ small cabbage, finely chopped

8-10 French beans, finely chopped

1 small onion, finely chopped

Salt to taste

5 tablespoons cornflour

2 tablespoons refined four

2 teaspoons red chilli flakes

¼ teaspoon MSG (optional)

2 tablespoons fresh coriander, finely chopped

¼ teaspoon white pepper powder

1 teaspoon light soy sauce

Oil for deep-frying

Method

1. In a large bowl, combine the carrot, cauliflower, capsicum, cabbage, French beans, onion and salt. Set aside for ten to fifteen minutes.
2. Squeeze the vegetables to remove excess water.

3 Add three tablespoons of cornflour, the refined flour, chilli flakes, MSG, fresh coriander, white pepper powder and soy sauce to the vegetables and mix well.

4 Divide the mixture into sixteen equal portions and roll into balls. Shape each ball into two-inch long fingers. Dust the vegetable fingers with two tablespoons of cornflour.

5 Heat sufficient oil in a wok and deep-fry the fingers till golden and crisp. Drain on absorbent paper.

6 Serve hot, with Sichuan Sauce (page 93).

Sago-Potato Rolls

Ingredients

¾ cup sago

3 large potatoes, boiled and mashed

½ cup roasted and peeled peanuts, crushed

3 green chillies, chopped

1 inch ginger, chopped

1 tablespoon lemon juice

2-3 tablespoons chopped fresh coriander

Salt to taste

Oil for deep-frying

Method

1. Wash the sago and soak in water for at least one hour. If in a hurry, soak the sago in hot water till the grains swell.
2. Squeeze out and place in a large bowl. Add the potatoes, peanuts, green chillies, ginger, lemon juice, fresh coriander and salt and mix well.
3. Add a little water if necessary and make a dough. Let it stand for a few minutes.
4. Divide the dough into eight equal portions and shape into oval rolls.
5. Heat sufficient oil in a *kadai* till medium hot.

6. Slide in four rolls at a time and deep-fry till golden.

7. Drain on absorbent paper. Serve hot with Green Chutney (page 92).

Chef's Tip: For a non-vegetarian version, you can substitute cooked minced meat (*keema*) for the mashed potatoes.

Corn Fritters

Ingredients

1½ cups sweetcorn kernels

6-8 garlic cloves, crushed

3 tablespoons chopped fresh coriander

3 fresh red chillies, chopped

2-3 spring onions, chopped

1 tablespoon light soy sauce

¾ cup rice flour

2 eggs, lightly beaten

¼ teaspoon black pepper powder

Salt to taste

Oil for shallow-frying

Method

1. Place the sweetcorn in a large bowl; add the garlic, fresh coriander, red chillies, spring onions, soy sauce, rice flour, eggs, pepper powder, salt and four tablespoons of water and mix well. The mixture should be firm enough to hold its shape, but not stiff.

2. Heat the oil in a frying pan; add spoonfuls of the corn mixture, gently spreading each dollop with the back of the spoon to make a round fritter.

3. Fry for one or two minutes on each side. Drain on absorbent paper. Serve hot with sweet chilli sauce.

Triple-Decker Sandwiches

Ingredients

12 slices day-old bread

1½ cups cream cheese

1 cup cheese spread

A few iceberg lettuce leaves

3-4 cucumbers, peeled and sliced

4 medium potatoes, boiled, peeled and sliced

Salt to taste

Black pepper powder to taste

3-4 tomatoes, sliced

5-6 pickled gherkins, sliced

1 teaspoon crushed red chillies

Method

1. Mix together the cream cheese and cheese spread together to make a smooth paste.
2. Spread a portion of the cheese paste on one slice of bread. Top with a lettuce leaf and cover with a layer of cucumber and potato slices.
3. Sprinkle salt and pepper powder and cover with another slice of bread.
4. Spread a generous portion of the cream cheese paste over the top of the second slice of bread.
5. Top with a few lettuce leaves, followed by tomato slices. Arrange sliced gherkins over the tomato and sprinkle with red chilli flakes.
6. Spread a portion of the cream cheese on the third slice and place it over the tomato layer with the cream cheese side facing downwards.
7. Cut the triple-layered sandwich diagonally into two triangles and serve immediately.
8. Repeat the process for the remaining sandwiches.

Sandwich Dhokla

Ingredients

1 cup rice

¼ cup skinless split black gram

¼ cup skimmed milk sour yogurt

Salt to taste

2 teaspoons ginger paste

1½ teaspoons green chilli paste

½ teaspoon soda bicarbonate

1 tablespoon lemon juice

½ cup thick Green Chutney (page 92)

2 tablespoons chopped fresh coriander

Method

1. Dry-roast the rice and the black gram over medium heat for four or five minutes. Cool and grind into a moderately coarse powder.
2. Place the powder in a bowl. Add the yogurt and one and a half cups of warm water. Mix thoroughly to make a smooth batter of pouring consistency. Stir in the salt.
3. Leave the batter to ferment for eight to ten hours. Add the ginger paste and green chilli paste to the batter and mix well.
4. Boil some water in a pressure cooker. Pour half the batter in a separate

bowl. In a small bowl, mix one-fourth teaspoon of soda bicarbonate and half a tablespoon of lemon juice.

5. Add to the batter and whisk well.Repeat this procedure for the remaining batter just before putting it into the steamer.
6. Pour the batter into a *thali* and place it in the pressure cooker. Steam without the weight for eight to ten minutes.
7. Test for doneness with a knife. If the knife comes out clean, it is cooked. Remove from the cooker and spread the green chutney over the *dhokla* while hot.
8. Pour the remaining batter over the chutney and steam again for ten minutes.
9. Remove from the cooker, cool slightly, and garnish with fresh coriander. Cut into desired shapes and serve hot.

Amritsari Paneer Pakore

Ingredients

400 grams cottage cheese, cut into 1-inch cubes

½ cup Green Chutney (page 92)

2½ cups gram flour

2 teaspoons carom seeds

1 teaspoon ginger-garlic paste

1½ teaspoons red chilli powder

Salt to taste

1 tablespoon lemon juice

Oil for deep-frying

Method

1. Slit each cottage cheese cube without cutting through. Spread the green chutney in the slit and set aside.
2. Mix the gram flour with one cup of water along with carom seeds, ginger-garlic paste, chilli powder, salt and lemon juice to make a smooth batter.
3. Heat sufficient oil in a *kadai*. Dip the sandwiched cottage cheese cubes in the batter and deep-fry till golden brown.
4. Drain on absorbent paper. Serve hot with tomato ketchup or chutney of your choice.

Pav Bhaji Roll-Ups

Ingredients

4 tortillas

8 lettuce leaves

Pav bhaji

3 tablespoons oil

2 medium onions, chopped

3-4 green chillies, chopped

2 teaspoons ginger paste

2 teaspoons garlic paste

4 medium tomatoes, chopped

1 medium green capsicum, chopped

¼ cup shelled green peas, boiled and mashed lightly

¼ small cauliflower, grated

4 medium potatoes, boiled and grated

1½ tablespoons *pav bhaji masala*

Salt to taste

2 tablespoons chopped fresh coriander

Onion-cheese mixture

1 large onion, sliced

½ teaspoon chilli powder

2 large tomatoes, seeded and sliced

1 cup grated processed cheese

Method

1. To make the *pav bhaji*, heat the oil in a pan and add three-fourth of the onions. Sauté till light brown. Add the green chillies, ginger paste and garlic paste and sauté for half a minute. Add half the tomatoes and cook over medium heat, stirring continuously, for three to four minutes, or till the oil separates from the *masala*.

2. Add the capsicum, peas, cauliflower, potatoes and one and a half cups of water. Bring to a boil and simmer for ten minutes, pressing with the back of the ladle a few times, till all the vegetables are completely mashed.

3. Add the *pav bhaji masala*, salt and the remaining tomatoes. Cook over medium heat for two minutes, stirring continuously. Transfer the *bhaji* to a *kadai* and simmer for five to ten minutes, stirring often, till all the moisture evaporates and the *bhaji* is quite dry. Add the chopped fresh coriander and mix. Transfer to a bowl and set aside.

4. Mix all the ingredients for the onion-cheese mixture together. Heat a *tawa* and lightly warm the tortillas on both sides. Place a warmed tortilla on a square piece of aluminium foil. Spread one-fourth of the *bhaji* over the tortilla and generously sprinkle one-fourth of the onion-cheese mixture over it. Place two lettuce leaves at one end of the tortilla and roll up tightly. Wrap in the foil and serve.

Three-Flavoured Popcorn

Sweet

Ingredients

½ cup dried corn kernels

¾ cup brown sugar

1 tablespoon oil

Method

1. Mix together the oil, brown sugar and corn kernels in a microwave-safe bowl.
2. Cover and cook on HIGH (100%) for six minutes, stirring once after three minutes.

Savoury

Ingredients

½ cup dried corn kernels

1 tablespoon oil

2 tablespoons cheese powder

1½ tablespoons red chilli flakes

Method

1. Mix together the oil and corn kernels in a microwave-safe bowl. Cover and cook on HIGH (100%) for six minutes, stirring once after three minutes.
2. Remove, add the cheese powder and chilli flakes and toss.

Tomato Flavour

Ingredients

½ cup dried corn kernels

1 tablespoon oil

1 tablespoon tomato powder

Salt to taste

Method

1. Mix the oil and corn kernels in a microwave-safe bowl.
2. Cover and cook on HIGH (100%) for six minutes, stirring once after three minutes.
3. Remove, add the tomato powder and salt to taste and toss.

Chef's Tip: Try out an interesting combination of all the flavours namely caramel, chilli-cheese and tomato. It happened to me once accidentally!

Crispy Wontons

Ingredients

24 Wonton Wrappers (see below)

2 tablespoons oil + for deep-frying

4-6 garlic cloves, finely chopped

2 spring onions, finely chopped

2 medium green capsicums, finely chopped

8-10 French beans, finely chopped

2 medium carrots, finely chopped

½ small cabbage, finely chopped

½ teaspoon white pepper powder

Salt to taste

¼ teaspoon MSG (optional)

1 teaspoon light soy sauce

Method

1. Heat two tablespoons of oil in a wok or pan; add the garlic and stir-fry for half a minute. Add the spring onions, capsicums, French beans, carrots and cabbage and continue to stir-fry for a couple of minutes longer, stirring and tossing continuously.

2 Add the white pepper powder, salt, MSG and soy sauce and cook for half a minute. Take the pan off the heat and set aside to cool.

3 Divide the prepared filling into twenty-four equal portions. Place a portion of filling in the centre of each wonton wrapper; moisten the edges with a little water, fold in half diagonally, twist the ends and press lightly to stick together.

4 Heat the oil in a wok and deep-fry the wontons for two to three minutes, or until crisp and golden brown. Drain on absorbent paper. Serve hot with Sichuan Sauce (page 93).

Wonton Wrappers

Knead 2 cups of refined flour with ½ cup warm water to make a firm dough. Roll the dough into a large thin square sheet, about 1 mm thick. Cut into 3-inch squares and use as required.

Chatpata Chiwda

Ingredients

250 grams nylon beaten rice

4 tablespoons oil

25 curry leaves

3 green chillies, broken into half

1 tablespoon sesame seeds

½ cup peanuts

2 tablespoons roasted Bengal gram

¼ cup thinly sliced dried coconut

½ teaspoon turmeric powder

½ teaspoon red chilli powder

2 tablespoons powdered sugar

Salt to taste

Method

1. Dry-roast the beaten rice in a *kadai* over medium heat till crisp. Transfer to a bowl and set aside.

2. Heat the oil in the same *kadai*; add the curry leaves, green chillies, sesame seeds, peanuts, roasted Bengal gram and dried coconut and sauté over low heat till they change colour.

3. Stir in the turmeric powder and chilli powder.
4. Add the beaten rice and mix gently so that the rice flakes do not break.
5. Sprinkle powdered sugar and salt and mix well.
6. Remove from heat and set aside to cool.
7. Place in an airtight jar. This *chiwda* has a long shelf life.

Paneer Capsicum Pakore

Ingredients

250 grams cottage cheese, cut into 1-inch squares

4 medium green capsicums, cut into 1-inch squares

½ medium bunch (125 grams) fresh coriander, chopped

½ medium bunch (125 grams) fresh mint, chopped

2 green chillies, chopped

½ tablespoon lemon juice

Salt to taste

Oil for deep-frying

Batter

½ inch ginger, chopped

2 garlic cloves, chopped

2 green chillies, chopped

1 cup gram flour

3 tablespoons cornflour

½ teaspoon baking powder

¼ teaspoon turmeric powder

1 teaspoon red chillies, crushed

Salt to taste

1 tablespoon lemon juice

1 tablespoon oil

To serve

2 teaspoons *chaat masala*

1 teaspoon red chilli powder

Method

1. To make the green chutney, grind together the fresh coriander, fresh mint and two green chillies to a fine paste. Add the lemon juice and salt to taste.

2. For the batter, separately grind together the ginger, garlic and two green chillies to a fine paste. Mix together the gram flour, cornflour, baking powder, turmeric powder, crushed red chillies, ginger-garlic-green chilli paste and salt in a bowl. Add the lemon juice and oil and mix. Add half a cup of water to make a thick batter.

3. Spread the green chutney on either side of the cottage cheese square. Stick the green capsicum squares on both sides of the cottage cheese square. In a bowl, mix the *chaat masala* and chilli powder.

4. Heat sufficient oil in a *kadai*. Dip the sandwiched cottage cheese squares in the batter and deep-fry till golden. Drain the *pakore* on absorbent paper. Cut into two halves. Place on a serving plate. Sprinkle the dry *masala* and serve hot.

Paneer Frankie

Ingredients

300 grams skimmed milk cottage cheese, cut into ½-inch cubes

1 cup wholewheat flour

Salt to taste

3 medium onions, roughly chopped

3 medium tomatoes, chopped

1 tablespoon ginger paste

1 tablespoon garlic paste

1 teaspoon Kashmiri chilli powder

½ teaspoon turmeric powder

2 teaspoons coriander powder (optional)

2 tablespoons lemon juice

To serve

8 teaspoons Green Chutney (page 92)

2 medium onions, sliced

Method

1. Mix the wholewheat flour and salt, add sufficient water and knead into a firm dough. Cover and set aside for about fifteen minutes.

2. Heat a non-stick pan, add the roughly chopped onions, tomatoes, ginger paste, garlic paste, salt, chilli powder, turmeric powder and coriander powder, and stir.

3. Cook till everything blends well and the excess moisture has dried up. Add the lemon juice, mix and take off the heat.

4. Add the cottage cheese cubes and mix lightly. Divide the filling into eight equal portions and set aside.

5. Divide the dough into eight equal balls and roll into *rotis*.

6. Heat a *tawa*, place a *roti* on it and cook till both the sides are evenly cooked.

7. Spread a teaspoon of green chutney all over the *roti*. Place a portion of cottage cheese mixture on one side. Sprinkle some sliced onions over it and roll up the *roti*.

8. Wrap in aluminum foil and serve immediately.

Paushtik Poha

Ingredients

2 cups beaten rice

½ cup soya granules

1 tablespoon oil

1 teaspoon cumin seeds

3 green chillies, finely chopped

8-10 curry leaves

½ teaspoon turmeric powder

2 medium onions, finely chopped

½ cup roasted peanuts

Salt to taste

2 tablespoons lemon juice

¼ cup fresh coriander, finely chopped

Method

1. Place the beaten rice in a colander, pour three to four cups of water evenly over to moisten the rice flakes. Drain well.

2. Wash the soya granules with warm water or alternatively soak in one cup of water for fifteen to twenty minutes. Drain and set aside.

3. Heat the oil in a non-stick pan and add the cumin seeds. Stir-fry briefly.
4. Add the chopped green chillies, curry leaves, turmeric powder and chopped onions. Stir-fry for two minutes on medium heat.
5. Add the soya granules and sprinkle with a quarter cup of water. Cook, covered, on low heat for five minutes. Stir well.
6. Add the beaten rice and toss over medium heat till heated through.
7. Add the roasted peanuts, salt and lemon juice. Toss well to mix.
8. Serve immediately, garnished with chopped fresh coriander.

Chatpati Shankerpali

Ingredients

2 cups savoury *shankerpali*, crushed

1 large onion, chopped

1 large tomato, seeded and chopped

3 green chillies, chopped

1 small unripe green mango, chopped

¼ cup *masala chana dal*

½ cup *tikha sev*

3 tablespoons chopped fresh coriander

4 teaspoons Green Chutney (page 92)

1½ tablespoons Date and Tamarind Chutney (page 92)

1 teaspoon lemon juice

Salt to taste

Method

1. In a large bowl, combine the crushed *shankerpali*, onion, tomato, green chillies, green mango, *masala chana dal* and *tikha sev* and toss to mix well.

2. Add the fresh coriander, green chutney, date and tamarind chutney, lemon juice and salt and toss again.

3. Spoon into four individual bowls and serve immediately.

Spinach And Cheese Idlis

Ingredients

½ cup skinless split black gram

1 cup *idli rawa*

Salt to taste

8-10 spinach leaves

¼ cup grated processed cheese

½ teaspoon crushed black peppercorns

Method

1. Soak the black gram and *idli rawa* separately for three to four hours.
2. Drain and grind the black gram, sprinkling water as required, to make a smooth, spongy batter.
3. Drain the *idli rawa* and add it with the salt to the black gram batter and mix thoroughly with your hands, using a whipping motion so that the batter is mixed well.
4. Place the batter in a large pan or bowl, cover tightly and rest in a warm place for eight hours, or overnight.
5. Blanch the spinach leaves in boiling water for two to three minutes.

6. Reserve a few leaves and purée the rest. Shred the reserved leaves.
7. Add the spinach purée to the *idli* batter and mix well. Pour into lightly-greased *idli* moulds, top with the shredded spinach leaves and grated cheese.
8. Sprinkle crushed peppercorns and steam till the *idlis* are done.
9. Serve with chilli sauce or chilli-garlic sauce.

Garden Vegetable Rolls

Ingredients

8 lettuce leaves, roughly torn

2 large cucumbers, thinly sliced

2 large tomatoes, thinly sliced

4 wholewheat hot dog rolls

2 tablespoons butter

Salt to taste

8-10 black peppercorns, freshly ground

2 tablespoons mustard paste

Thousand Island Dressing

4 tablespoons eggless mayonnaise

1 tablespoon tomato ketchup

1 teaspoon Tabasco sauce

1 jalapeño chilli, chopped

1 pickled onion, chopped

1 pickled gherkin, chopped

Method

1. To prepare the Thousand Island dressing mix all the ingredients well.
2. Slit the buns without cutting through. Spread a little butter on both sides.
3. Arrange the lettuce, cucumber and tomato slices evenly on one half of each roll.
4. Sprinkle a little salt and ground pepper.
5. Drizzle a little mustard paste and Thousand Island dressing.
6. Cover with the second half and serve immediately.

Kanda Bhajia

Ingredients

4 large onions, sliced

Salt to taste

Oil for deep-frying

1 cup gram flour

1 teaspoon red chilli powder

Method

1. Slice the onions Add salt and squeeze to extract excess water. Heat the oil in a *kadai* till very hot.

2. Add the gram flour and chilli powder to the onion and mix. Do not add any water.

3. Drop portions of onion mixture into the hot oil. If the *bhajia* stick together, try to separate them. Drain when the *bhajia* are half done.

4. Just before serving, refry the *bhajia* in very hot oil till golden. Drain on absorbent paper and serve hot with chutney.

Chef's Tip: Slice the onions just before frying to make crisp *bhajia*.

Mawa Cupcakes

Ingredients

1½ cups refined flour

1½ tablespoons *mawa*, crumbled

150 grams butter, softened

¾ cup powdered sugar

5 tablespoons milk powder

2 tablespoons cornflour

1 teaspoon baking powder

1 teaspoon soda bicarbonate

¼ teaspoon green cardamom powder

¼ cup buttermilk

2 tablespoons milk

Method

1. Preheat the oven to 180°C/350°F/ Gas Mark 4. Grease twelve moulds or paper cups.
2. Cream the butter and powdered sugar in a bowl with a wooden spoon till light and fluffy.
3. Sift the milk powder into the bowl and continue to mix. Add the *mawa* and mix again.
4. Sift the flour, cornflour, baking powder, soda bicarbonate and cardamom powder together into the bowl and mix.

5. Add the buttermilk to adjust the consistency. If the batter is still too thick add a little milk and mix.

6. Pour the batter into the greased moulds or paper cups. Tap the moulds lightly to level the batter. Bake for thirty minutes.

7. Remove from the oven and place on a wire rack to cool before unmoulding. Serve warm or cold.

Makes 12 cupcakes

Eggless Brownies

Ingredients

100 grams dark chocolate, grated

1⅓ cups refined flour

2 teaspoons baking powder

130 grams butter

1 cup + 1½ tablespoons caster sugar

1 teaspoon vanilla essence

½ cup walnut kernels, chopped

Method

1. Preheat an oven to 180°C/350°F/ Gas Mark 4. Grease an eight-inch square cake tin.
2. Sift the flour and baking powder together. Melt the chocolate and butter in a double-boiler, or in a large microwave-safe bowl, uncovered, in the microwave oven on HIGH (100%) for one minute.
3. Beat in the sugar and vanilla essence and blend well. Add the sifted flour and walnuts and mix well.
4. Pour the mixture into the tin and bake for twenty-five to thirty minutes. Remove from the oven and place on a wire rack to cool. Cut into squares and serve.

Makes 16 brownies

Zesty Lemon Cake

Ingredients

1¾ cups refined flour

Grated rind of 1 lemon

3 tablespoons lemon juice

1 teaspoon soda bicarbonate

2 teaspoons baking powder

100 grams butter + for greasing

½ cup powdered sugar

1¼ cups yogurt

Topping

3 tablespoons lemon juice

3 tablespoons sugar

Method

1. Sift together the flour, soda bicarbonate and baking powder into a bowl.
2. In a separate bowl, cream together the butter and powdered sugar. Add the yogurt, lemon rind and lemon juice and mix well.
3. Add the flour, a little at a time, and fold into the batter.
4. Heat a pressure cooker with some water and place a perforated plate in it.
5. Grease an eight-inch round cake tin lightly with butter and pour the cake batter into the tin.

6. Place the tin on the base in the pressure cooker. Remove the gasket and cover the cooker with the lid without the weight.

7. Cook for thirty to thirty-five minutes. Remove when done.

8. For the topping, put the sugar and three tablespoons of water into a pan and heat till the sugar dissolves. Stir in the lemon juice.

9. Pour the syrup over the hot cake Cool the cake in the tin, slice and serve.

Makes one 8-inch round cake.

Crunchy Peanut Cookies

Ingredients

½ cup peanut butter

2 tablespoons crushed roasted peanuts

¾ cup + 1 tablespoon refined flour

¼ teaspoon soda bicarbonate

½ teaspoon cinnamon powder

¾ cup + 1 tablespoon caster sugar

½ cup rolled (porridge) oats

¼ cup + 1 tablespoon desiccated coconut

1 teaspoon grated lemon rind

1 tablespoon golden syrup

Method

1. Preheat an oven to 180°C/350°F/ Gas Mark 4. Grease a baking tray.
2. Sift together the flour, soda bicarbonate and cinnamon powder into a bowl.
3. Add the sugar, oats, desiccated coconut and lemon rind and mix well.
4. Add the peanut butter, crushed peanuts, golden syrup and approximately two tablespoons of water and mix into a soft dough.
5. Knead gently on a lightly floured surface until smooth.

Crunchy Peanut Cookies

Ingredients

½ cup peanut butter

2 tablespoons crushed roasted peanuts

¾ cup + 1 tablespoon refined flour

¼ teaspoon soda bicarbonate

½ teaspoon cinnamon powder

¾ cup + 1 tablespoon caster sugar

½ cup rolled (porridge) oats

¼ cup + 1 tablespoon desiccated coconut

1 teaspoon grated lemon rind

1 tablespoon golden syrup

Method

1. Preheat an oven to 180°C/350°F/ Gas Mark 4. Grease a baking tray.
2. Sift together the flour, soda bicarbonate and cinnamon powder into a bowl.
3. Add the sugar, oats, desiccated coconut and lemon rind and mix well.
4. Add the peanut butter, crushed peanuts, golden syrup and approximately two tablespoons of water and mix into a soft dough.
5. Knead gently on a lightly floured surface until smooth.

6. Wrap the dough in cling film and refrigerate for about thirty minutes.

7. Divide the dough in half and roll out each half between sheets of greaseproof paper into a quarter-inch thick rectangle.

8. Cut into rounds with a two-and-a-half-inch round cookie cutter. Place well apart on the baking tray. Bake for about fifteen minutes or until light golden brown.

9. Remove from the oven and transfer the cookies to a wire rack to cool. Store in an airtight container.

Makes 35 cookies

Kela Halwa

Ingredients

2 cups ripe Rajali banana pulp

1 cup sugar

4 tablespoons pure ghee

Oil for greasing

Method

1. In a thick-bottomed vessel, cook together the banana pulp and sugar, stirring all the time till the mixture starts thickening.
2. Add two tablespoons of ghee and continue to cook, stirring continuously.

   As it thickens some more, add the rest of the ghee and continue to cook stirring continuously.
3. To test for doneness, roll a small quantity into a ball, if it does not stick to the palms, it is done.
4. Pour the mixture onto a greased *thali* and spread evenly with a greased rolling pin or the back of a flat ladle.
5. Cut into square or diamond-shaped pieces when still hot, but do not separate them. Set aside to cool. Separate the pieces and store.

Note: If Rajali bananas are not available you can use green-skinned ripe bananas.

Honey Crisps

Ingredients

2 tablespoons honey

½ cup refined flour

150 grams unsalted butter

¼ cup sugar

2½ cups (85 grams) cornflakes

Method

1. Preheat an oven to 190°C/375°F/ Gas Mark 5. Grease a baking tray.
2. Cream together the butter, sugar and honey in a bowl.
3. Add the flour and cornflakes. If necessary, add a little more honey and mix into a dough.
4. Divide the dough into twelve equal portions and roll into balls. Flatten slightly.
5. Place well apart on the greased baking tray as the cookies will spread while baking. Bake for fifteen minutes.
6. Remove from the oven and transfer the cookies to a wire rack to cool. Store in an airtight container.

Makes 12 cookies

Nankhatai

Ingredients

2½ cups refined flour

½ cup gram flour

1 cup ghee

1¾ cups powdered sugar

¼ cup yogurt

1 teaspoon baking ammonia (ammonium bicarbonate)

¼ teaspoon coarsely ground green cardamom seeds

Method

1. Cream the ghee and sugar together in a food processor.
2. Add the yogurt and process again. Rest the mixture for ten minutes.
3. Sift together the flour, gram flour and ammonia. Mix in the cardamom powder.
4. Add the flour mixture to the ghee and sugar mixture and process once more till well mixed.
5. Transfer the dough to a bowl and rest it for half an hour.

6. Preheat an oven to 180°C/350°F/Gas Mark 4. Grease a baking tray.
7. Divide the dough into thirty small balls and place them a small distance apart on the tray. Bake for twenty to twenty-five minutes.
8. Let the *nankhatais* cool on the tray for a while and transfer to wire racks to cool completely. Store in an airtight container.

Makes 30 nankhatais

Coconut Karanji

Ingredients

Pastry covering

1 cup refined flour

1½ tablespoons semolina

4 tablespoons ghee + for deep-frying

¼ cup milk

Stuffing

1 cup fresh grated coconut

15-20 raisins, chopped

1 cup powdered sugar

½ teaspoon green cardamom powder

Method

1. Sieve the refined flour into a bowl. Add the semolina and ghee and mix with your fingertips till the mixture resembles breadcrumbs. Knead into a semi-soft dough with the milk and sufficient water.
2. Cover the dough with a damp cloth and set aside for half an hour.
3. For the stuffing, roast the grated coconut in a thick-bottomed *kadai* till lightly browned.
4. Add the chopped raisins, powdered sugar and cardamom powder and mix well. Leave to cool.

5. Knead the dough once again and divide it into twelve small balls.
6. Roll out each ball into a circle and place it in a greased *karanji* mould.
7. Place a small portion of the prepared filling in the hollow. Moisten the edges with a little water, close the mould and press firmly.
8. Heat sufficient ghee in a *kadai* and fry the *karanjis* till crisp and golden brown on medium heat.
9. Drain on absorbent paper and allow to cool before storing in an airtight container.

Aloo Ka Halwa

Ingredients

6 medium potatoes, boiled, peeled and grated

½ cup ghee

1 cup milk

1½ cups powdered sugar

1 teaspoon green cardamom powder

½ cup assorted nuts, chopped

Method

1. Heat the ghee in a heavy-bottomed pan. Add the grated potatoes and sauté well. The longer you sauté the better the *halwa* tastes.
2. Stir continuously as the potatoes tend to stick to the bottom.
3. Add the milk and powdered sugar and mix well. Cook till the sugar dissolves completely and the ghee starts to separate.
4. Add the cardamom powder and assorted nuts and mix well. Serve warm.

Doodhi Halwa

Ingredients

600 grams bottle gourd, peeled and grated

2 tablespoons ghee

7 tablespoons sugar

¼ cup grated *khoya/mawa*

¼ teaspoon green cardamom powder

1 tablespoon raisins

5-6 cashew nuts, chopped

5-6 almonds, blanched and slivered

Method

1. Heat the ghee in a pressure cooker. Add the grated bottle gourd and sauté for five minutes. Add the sugar, seal the cooker with the lid and cook over medium heat till the pressure is released three times (three whistles).

2. Remove the lid when the pressure has reduced completely and add the *khoya* and cardamom powder.

3. Cook, stirring continuously, for two or three minutes, or till the excess liquid evaporates.

4. Add the raisins, cashew nuts and almonds and continue to cook for two more minutes. Serve hot or at room temperature.

Gur Ki Meethi Kadak Puri

Ingredients

¾ cup grated jaggery

2 cups wholewheat flour

A pinch of green cardamom powder (optional)

¼ cup pure ghee + for deep-frying

Method

1. Mix the jaggery with three-fourth cup of water in a pan and heat the mixture gently over a very low heat till the jaggery melts completely. Strain.
2. Place the flour in a bowl and add the cardamom powder. Rub in the pure ghee till the mixture resembles breadcrumbs.
3. Add the jaggery mixture and knead into a stiff dough. Cover with a damp cloth and allow the dough to rest for half an hour.
4. Divide the dough into sixteen equal portions and shape into balls. Roll out into three-inch *puris* and prick on both sides with a fork.
5. Heat the ghee in a *kadai* and deep-fry the *puris* in moderately hot ghee till golden and crisp. Drain on absorbent paper. Serve hot or cold.

Saeb Ka Halwa

Ingredients

2 cups grated apples

¾ cup sugar

½ cup *khoya/mawa*, grated

¼ teaspoon green cardamom powder

2 tablespoons chopped assorted nuts

Method

1. Cook the grated apples with sugar in a thick-bottomed *kadai* till the sugar melts.
2. Add the *khoya* and cook over low heat until the *khoya* melts.
3. Continue to cook over low heat, stirring continuously, until the moisture dries up. Stir in the cardamom powder.
4. Decorate with the assorted nuts and serve hot.

Pineapple Sheera

Ingredients

1 small (250 grams) pineapple, peeled and chopped

1 cup semolina

1 cup ghee

A pinch of saffron

1 cup sugar

5-6 cashew nuts

5-6 almonds

Method

1. Heat the ghee in a pan; add the semolina and cook, stirring continuously, till golden brown. Add the saffron and mix.
2. Add the pineapple and cook for another two or three minutes.
3. Stir in two cups of water; cover and cook over medium heat for three minutes.
4. Add the sugar and keep stirring till all the moisture evaporates and the semolina is cooked completely.
5. Garnish with cashew nuts and almonds and serve hot.

ANNEXURE

Date And Tamarind Chutney

Wash, stone and chop 15-20 dates. Dry-roast 2 teaspoons cumin seeds and ¼ teaspoon fennel seeds. Cool and grind to a powder. Cook dates, 1 cup tamarind pulp, cumin and fennel powder, ½ cup jaggery, 2 teaspoons red chilli powder, 1 teaspoon dried ginger powder, black salt, salt and four cups of water till thick.

Green Chutney

Grind together 1 cup fresh coriander, ½ cup fresh mint, 2-3 green chillies, black salt to taste, ¼ teaspoon sugar and 1 tablespoon lemon juice to a smooth paste, using a little water if required.

Red Chilli-Garlic Chutney

Soak 10 dried red chillies in 1½ cups of water for half an hour. Drain and grind with 12 large garlic cloves, and 2 teaspoons lemon juice to a fine paste. Add sea salt and 1 teaspoon cumin powder and mix well.

Sichuan Sauce

Ingredients

10-12 dried red chillies

½ cup oil

10 garlic cloves, peeled and finely chopped

2 green chillies, finely chopped

2 spring onions, finely chopped

1 inch fresh ginger, peeled and grated

2-3 inch celery stalk, finely chopped

3 tablespoons tomato ketchup

Salt to taste

2 teaspoons white vinegar

Method

1. Boil the red chillies in one cup of water for five to seven minutes. Drain, cool and grind to a fine paste. Heat the oil in a pan, add the garlic, green chillies, spring onions and the ginger and sauté for one minute.
2. Add the red chilli paste and continue to sauté for a few more seconds. Add the celery, tomato ketchup and salt and stir well to mix.
3. Stir in the vinegar; simmer for one minute. Take the pan off the heat when the oil rises to the surface. Cool and store.

Note: Sichuan sauce will keep for a month if there is sufficient oil covering the surface.

GLOSSARY

English	Hindi
Almonds	badam
Apple	saeb
Banana	kela
Basil, fresh	tulsi ke patte
Basil seeds	tukmaria/subza
Bean sprouts	ankurit moong
Beans	moong
Bengal gram, roasted	dalia
Black gram, skinless split	dhuli urad dal
Bottle gourd	lauki/doodhi
Brown gram	matki/moth
Butter	makkhan
Buttermilk	chhach
Cabbage	patta gobhi
Capsicum, green	hari Shimla mirch
Cardamom, green	chhoti elaichi
Carom seeds	ajwain
Carrot	gajar
Cashew nuts	kaju
Cauliflower	phoolgobhi
Chilies, fresh red	taazi lal mirch

English	Hindi
Chillies, dried red	sookhi lal mirch
Chillies, green	hari mirch
Cinnamon	dalchini
Coconut, desiccated	khopra ka bareek choora
Coconut, dried	khopra
Coconut, fresh	nariyal
Coriander, fresh	hara dhania
Corn kernels	makai ke dane
Cottage cheese	paneer
Cream	malai
Cucumber	kakdi
Cumin seeds	jeera
Curry leaves	kadipatta
Dates	khajoor
Fennel seeds	saunf
French beans	farsi
Ginger, dried	sonth
Gram flour	besan
Honey	shahad
Jaggery	gur

English	Hindi
Lemon	nimbu
Lemon rind	nimbu ka chilka
Lettuce	salad ke patte
Mango, ripe	aam
Mango, unripe green	keri
Melon seeds	magaz
Mint, fresh	pudina ke taazi pattiyan
Mustard seeds	rai
Nutmeg	jaiphal
Oats	jaee
Onions	pyaaz
Papaya	papita
Peanuts	moongphali
Peanuts, spiced	masala moongphali
Peas, fresh green	taazi hari matar
Peppercorns, black	kali mirch
Peppercorns, white	safed mirch
Pineapple	ananas
Pistachios	pista
Pomegranate kernels	anar ke dane

English	Hindi
Poppy seeds	khuskhus
Raisins	kishmish
Refined flour	maida
Rice, beaten	poha
Saffron	kesar
Sago	sabudana
Salt, black	kala namak
Salt, sea	samudri namak
Semolina	rawa/sooji
Sesame seeds, white	safed til
Spinach	palak
Spring onions	hara pyaaz
Star anise	chakri phool/ badiyan
Sugar	cheeni
Tamarind pulp	imli ka gooda
Tea leaves	chai ki pattiyan
Tomato	tamatar
Turmeric	haldi
Vinegar	sirka
Walnut	akhrot
Wholewheat flour	atta
Yogurt	dahi

Books by Sanjeev Kapoor

Small Format

Title	MRP ₹
The Party Food Cookbook	110
Non-Vegetarian Soups and Salads	99
Best of Paneer: A collection of Vegetarian Recipes	99
Cocktail Snacks	99
Desi Murgh	99
Curries	99
South Indian Snacks	99
Roti-Paranthe	110
Vegetarian Breakfast Bonanza	125
Scrumptious Vegetarian Salads	99
Delicious Vegetarian Soups	99
Vegetarian After-School Snacks	125
Vegetarian Soups	125
Recipes for Non-Stick Cookware	125
Vegetarian Cooking with Dahi	110
Go Green	99
Healthy Tasty Recipes	99
Monsoon Medley	99
Chill Out! Summer Eats & Treats	99
Mango Masti	99
Tawa-Handi Recipes	125
Sunday Specials	125
Simple Home Baking	110
Chai-Nashta	125
Mirch Mazaa	125
Sweet Temptations	110
Dal-Roti	99
Desi Sabziyan	110
Pickles, Chutneys 'n' More	110
Say Cheese!	99
Mushroom Mania	99
Noodles and Pasta	110
Makai Magic	99
Eggs	99
Desi Aloo	99
Dahi	125
Rice, Biryani and Pulao	125
Vegetarian Rice, Biryani and Pulao	125
Kadai Cooking	110
Pressure Cooking	99
No-Oil Recipes	99
No-Oil Vegetarian Recipes	110
Street Food	125
Desi Mutton	95
Thai Cooking	99
Paneer	110
Italian Cooking	99
Drinks and Mocktails	125
Vegetarian Breakfasts	125
Salads	125
Non-Vegetarian Recipes From Around The World	99
Vegetarian Recipes From Around The World	110
Seafood	125
Chicken Recipes	125
Punjabi	99
Chinese Non-Vegetarian Cooking	110
Chinese Vegetarian Cooking	99
Microwave Desi Cooking	110
Sweet Encounters	99
Soups, Salads and Sandwiches	110
Vegetarian Snacks and Starters	110
Non-Vegetarian Snacks and Starters	110

Big Format

Title	MRP ₹
The Yellow Chilli Cookbook	595
Mithai - Sweets for every celebration	295
Kitchen Library Eat Lite - Low-calorie Vegetarian Collection (set of 5 volumes)	485
Cooking with Love - Vegetarian Recipes from My Mother's Kitchen	295
Healthy Indian Cooking for Diabetes	345
100 Favourite Hand-Picked Recipes	595
Fun Food for Fussy Kids	350
Kitchen Library Vegetarian Collection (set of 5 volumes)	485
Simply Stylish - Entertaining at Home	395
Wedding Collection - Recipes for Newly-weds	1200
Dakshin Delights	295
Everyday Indian with Olive Oil	49
Marwari Vegetarian Cooking	295
Tandoori Cooking @ Home	275
Flavours of the Orient	250
Wrap 'N' Roll	350
Party Cooking	295
Dal and Kadhi	350
Chaat	350
T.V. Dinner	350
Cakes and Bakes	295
No-Oil Vegetarian Cooking	275
No-Oil Cooking	295
Konkan Cookbook	275
Simply Indian	275
Royal Hyderabadi Cooking	350
Best of Chinese Cooking	275
Microwave Cooking Made Easy	295
Khazana of Healthy Tasty Recipes	250
Any Time Temptations	295
Low Calorie Vegetarian Cookbook	295
Khana Khazana: Celebration of Indian Cookery	295
Khazana of Indian Vegetarian Recipes	275
Khazana of Indian Recipes	295

NEW RELEASES

Big Format

Title	MRP ₹
Everyday Cooking	295
Aah! Chocolate	595
Low-Salt Cookbook	195
Tiffins - Delicious and Healthy Khana for Dabba	295

Small Format

Title	MRP ₹
Iron-Rich Recipes	110
Vegetarian Finger Foods	110
Kabab Lajawab!	99
Vegetarian Recipes from Marwar	99
Noodles and Rice	99